!! AYUSHMAN BHAVA !!

A CONCISE DESCRIPTION OF AYURVEDA

DR. JAGADEESH PILLAI

Dedicated to everyone around me, with a prayer for their good health.

Contents

Contents

Contents

Prayer

Oṃ namāmi dhanvantariṃ ādidevama I

surāsura vandite pada padmam II

loke jarā ruk bhaya mṛtyu nāśanam I

dhatarmiśam vividha auṣadhinām II

I offer my salutations to you, Lord Dhanvantari, the incarnation of Lord Vishnu and the embodiment of Sudarshana Vasudev Dhanvantari. You hold in your hands the Kalasha filled with the elixir of immortality. Oh Lord, you can dispel all fears and diseases, protect the three worlds, and be the benevolent guardian of all living beings. You are the Lord of Ayurveda and the manifestation of Lord Vishnu, the ultimate healer of all creatures. May your divine grace bring us health and longevity.

About The Author

Dr. Jagadeesh Pillai four times Guinness World Record holder, a voracious reader, writer, and true research scholar was born in Varanasi, the abode of Lord Shiva. He is Ph.D. in Vedic Science. He is a multi-faceted polymath with innate qualities, creative ideas and many remarkable achievements. Although his roots extend back to "Gods own Country"(Kerala), the residents of Varanasi feel proud of him and adore him as a child of Varanasi who caters to every individual in need without any expectations. A deep study into his profile reflects that he has added so many feathers to his cap which makes him quite unique. He is a four times Guinness Book of World Records Holder in the following subjects :

1. "Script to Screen" which he achieved by producing and directing a state of art animation film within the shortest time possible by breaking the earlier set record by Canadians. There are many national and international Awards and Recognitions to his credit.
2. Longest Line of Post Cards which he has done on the occasion of 163 years of Indian Postal Day by 16300 post cards. The event was also connected with a questionnaire about Indian Flag.
3. Largest Poster Awareness Campaign – This was achieved by designing an awareness campaign on the subject "Beti Bachao – Beti Padhao".
4. Largest Envelop – Towards tribute to Prime Minister's initiative 'Make in India' – he has created about 4000 sq meter envelop using waste papers.
5. Attempted by lighting 70000 candles on a 210 kg cake to

celebrate the 70th Indian Independence day recorded in World Records India.

6. Attempted a documentary on Dhamek Stupa of Sarnath dubbing in 17 languages, result is waiting from Guinness World Records.

He is versatile in Gita teaching. The young generation is fond of his Gita teaching and he has changed the life of many young through his continued motivational boost up and teachings.

He has composed and sung Gayatri Mantra in 1008 different tunes.

He has composed and sung Hanuman Chalisa in 108 different tunes.

He has composed and sung hundreds of Sanskrit Bhajans, Patriotic songs, etc.

He has written and directed so many short films and documentaries for awareness campaigns.

He has done voluntary services to UP Police and Kerala Police to spread awareness campaigns on the various issue through videos and photography.

He is on the path of authoring thousands of books on Indian culture, Indian Temples, and the life of extraordinary people.

It is hard to believe that he has produced and directed more than 100 Documentaries on a particular city (Varanasi) which is done by a single person.

He has helped and guided more than 25 boys and girls to achieve world records through various creative and innovative methods.

A multifaceted person who can apply the best of his intellect using the God-given blessings which have been showered upon every human being granting them an immense capacity to learn, experience, and experiment with many things and do wonders in this world of discrimination and disparities.

He is a teacher and a student at the same time who always learns every day and teaches every day. As a master, his weakness was that he never sticks to a particular subject. Perhaps this weakness gives him the strength to master any area which he came across.

Each of his days dawned with learning a new topic and he spend most of his time experimenting and researching it.

He is also a selfless social activist and a motivational speaker.

His life was full of struggle, ups and downs, and failures. But he never gave up and faced all his trials and tribulations full of confidence. Today he is a successful young man with a lot of enthusiasm and rich life experience.

He has sung full Ram Charita Manas 51 hours audio by his own composition. He has also sung the whole Bhagavad-

Gita in his own composition with a rhythmic background.

He has also sung "Lokah Samastha Sukhino Bhavantu" in 50 different languages.

Currently working on a detailed and scientific study on Veda, Upanishad, Puranas, Bhagavad Gita, etc.

He has composed and sung Hanuman Chalisa in 108 different compositions and Gayatri Mantra in 1008 different compositions.

Awards

Four Times Guinness World Records

Winner of Mahatma Gandhi Vishwa Shanti Puraskar

Mahatma Gandhi Global Peace Ambassador

Kashi Ratna Award

Dr. APJ Abdul Kalam Motivational Person of the Year 2017

Mother Teresa Award

Indira Gandhi Priyadarshini Award

Bharat Vikas Ratna Award

Udyog Ratna Award

Vigyan Prasar Award

Poorvanchal Ratn Samman

Preface

Ayurveda is an ancient Indian system of health and healing, often seen as one of the oldest forms of medicine. It has stood the test of time and continues to be used by many people today to support healthy habits and treat a wide range of illnesses and conditions. Ayurvedic knowledge rests on the belief that all life forms contain energy which needs to be in balance for optimal health. This book is intended to provide readers with an introduction to this system, exploring different aspects such as dietary habits, natural treatments, meditation practices, oils and herbs. By understanding the ways in which these elements can help restore harmony within oneself, readers will gain insight into how they can positively affect their well-being on both physical and mental levels.

This book is based on my notes while attempting to comprehend the ancient Indian medical system of Ayurveda. Through my research, I have gained a deeper understanding of this holistic approach to health and wellness. I hope that this book will provide readers with an insightful look into the principles of Ayurveda and how they can be applied to their own lives.

by : Dr. Jagadeesh Pillai (PhD in Vedic Science & Four Times Guinness World Record Holder)

CHAPTER ONE

AYURVEDA AN ALTERNATIVE MEDICINE

Ayurveda is an ancient system of alternative medicine deeply rooted in Indian culture, which has been practised since time immemorial. Ayurveda is composed of the Sanskrit words 'Ayur' meaning 'life' and 'Daya' meaning 'knowledge'. It is a holistic system of well-being and has served as an integral part of India's traditional healthcare for centuries.

This medical framework combines several insights from nature, such as elements of medicine from plants and minerals, yoga, massage, and meditation. It assigns special significance to diet, nutrition, the environment, and lifestyle, used to prevent and treat illness, bring balance to the body, and ultimately restore health. These remedies are based on the concept of balancing three distinctly different energizing forces of the 'doshas' - Vata, Pitta, and Kapha. Each person is said to have a unique combination of these different energies which can be managed by changes in diet and lifestyle to create harmony and balance.

Ayurvedic practitioners traditionally focus on treating the underlying cause of a problem, rather than treating the symptoms in isolation. Along with physical illness, Ayurveda treats the impact of mental and emotional issues, such as excess stress, anxiety, insomnia and depression. Ayurveda emphasizes the value of preventative health care and offers a wide range of remedies to optimise physical and emotional wellbeing. Many of these remedies - such as yoga, dietary amendments, पर्णाशरोग (A biennial herbal medicine from the foothills of the Himalayas often used to treat rheumatic and joint disorders), herbal remedies, and massage therapy - help to reduce and manage a wide range of health challenges.

Ayurveda also promotes spiritual exploration. Ancient Indian health traditions recognize that our physical and emotional health are connected to our spiritual life, with physical ailments thought to be related to imbalances in spiritual, mental and emotional states of health. Ayurvedic treatments, such as yoga and meditation, help to create balance and harmony in our lives.

Ayurveda is a holistic health system that has been used to prevent and treat physical and emotional ailments in the Indian subcontinent for centuries. This ancient system of medicine aims to restore our bodies back to the harmony of the natural environment and lifestyle, supporting our physical and emotional wellbeing. With the right balance of knowledge, nutrition, and lifestyle, Ayurveda effectively helps to maintain health and wellbeing for individuals and society.

"By cleansing the bodily humours, removing toxins, and strengthening the system, it is possible to achieve good health, longevity, and joy" - Charaka Samhita, Indian Ayurvedic text

CHAPTER TWO

LORD DHANVANTARI – AVATAR OF VISHNU

Dhanvantari is the Avatar of Vishnu, the Hindu God that is associated with Ayurveda. He is best known for bringing the knowledge of Ayurveda – the ancient Indian system of medicine and healing - to the world. Dhanvantari is revered as the patron deity of medicine and healing. He is seen to represent the healing arts, health, and longevity.

In Hindu mythology, Dhanvantari is said to have emerged from the Ocean of Milk or 'Ksheer-Sagar' when the devas (gods) and asuras (demons) were churning the primordial ocean for the 'amrita'; the divine nectar of immortality. While the devas and asuras were fighting, a shloka (sacred sentence) arose from the ocean and this was the form of Dhanvantari. He was holding a pot of Amrita (nectar of immortality) in one hand and a vedic scripture on Ayurveda in the other hand.

Dhanvantari is usually depicted as either a four-armed deity or, more commonly, a two-armed human figure with a white complexion. He is said to possess a beauty and serenity that radiates from him. He is usually depicted wearing a yellow or white dhoti (loin cloth) with a shawl draped around his body. In some images, he is seen with four arms, one with a pot of Amrita, one with a chakra or wheel and two with a conch and a mace or Kamandala. The wheel and the mace represent his two-fold powers - firstly, to diagnose and treat physical ailments, and secondly, to ease the suffering of mankind from all spiritual evil.

Dhanvantari is also associated with Ayurvedic principles and treatments. He is considered to be the creator of the Ayurvedic system of medicine and its treatments. He is seen as the protector of health and longevity, and is responsible for maintaining a balance between the body, mind and spirit. According to Hindu belief, Dhanvantari brings healing to all those who seek his guidance and blessing.

Dhanvantari is the traditional deity of festivals such as the 'Dhanteras' and is worshipped by many Hindus around the world. According to tradition, this holy day marks the start of Diwali, the Hindu Feast of Lights, and it is also an occasion when people make a special effort to please the gods. On this day, worshipers make offerings to Dhanvantari and pray for health, wellness and spiritual strength.

In modern times, Dhanvantari remains an important figure in Hinduism and is seen to represent the highest level of the healing arts. He is the deity of Ayurvedic healing and is dedicated to the works of health and longevity.

"Ayurveda is the foundation of life, the basis of all
therapies, and should be the first step in health treatment"
- Veda Vyasa, Ayurvedic scholar

CHAPTER THREE

THE THEORY AND PRACTICE OF AYURVEDA

Ayurveda is an ancient system of traditional Indian medicine. It dates back to around 600 BC and its practice consists of natural treatments such as herbs, yoga and meditation. While Ayurveda is still practiced in many countries today, some argue that the theories and practices of the system are pseudoscientific.

The main argument against the pseudoscientific nature of Ayurveda is the lack of scientific evidence to support its claims. Ayurveda is based on a holistic approach to healthcare, so it often advocates for natural remedies such as herbs, spices and massage. While natural remedies might be beneficial, there is little scientific proof to show that they are effective in treating serious medical conditions. Furthermore, some of the treatments proposed by Ayurveda are potentially dangerous and the dosages are often not properly regulated. Without scientific evidence, the efficacy of Ayurveda's treatments is highly questionable.

Another factor that contributes to the pseudoscientific nature of Ayurveda is its lack of standardization. Ayurveda does not have a centralized system of practice, meaning the remedies and advice given by different practitioners may vary widely. The lack of a standardized system to follow means that practitioners may use treatments that are not supported by scientific evidence, making it difficult to determine the safety and efficacy of their treatments.

Additionally, Ayurveda is also often criticized for its lack of transparency. The recipes used for various remedies are usually kept as trade secrets, meaning that even well-educated and experienced practitioners may not have a detailed understanding of the ingredients used in their treatments. This lack of transparency makes it difficult to evaluate the medical efficacy of the remedies.

Overall, while the practice of Ayurveda is still popular in many countries, the theories and practices behind the system are largely considered pseudoscientific. The lack of evidence to support its claims, the lack of standardization, and the opacity of the remedies used make it difficult to evaluate the safety and efficacy of its treatments. In order for practitioners to provide scientifically-sound treatments, further research into the underlying principles of Ayurveda is needed.

"Ayurveda is the science of healing the mind, body, and soul. It is based on the natural laws, and has been in existence since time immemorial" - Swami Sundara, Indian author

CHAPTER FOUR

AYURVEDIC PREPARATIONS & HERBAL COMPOUNDS

Ayurvedic preparations are medicinal formulations that have been around for thousands of years, and continue to be widely used to promote wellness and treat health conditions. These remedies typically combine herbs, spices, minerals and other natural ingredients in order to create powerful treatments that are tailored to the individual.

Ayurvedic preparations typically feature a combination of herbs, and these can vary from simple single-herb concoctions to complex blends of dozens of components. Each herb is believed to possess unique qualities and can be chosen for its ability to address individual constitutional imbalances. For example, herbs such as Ashwagandha, Brahmi and Triphala are often used in Ayurvedic remedies to promote a sense of wellbeing, reduce stress, and improve mental clarity. Other herbs such as Guggul, Amalaki and Shatavari are often used to address digestive issues and promote healthy metabolism.

The herbs themselves are typically combined in the form of powders, teas and extracts. Powders are usually used to make tablets and capsules. Teas allow for the infusion of herbs into hot water, whose steam is also believed to carry beneficial components of the herbs into the body. Extracts are concentrated in order to obtain the strongest medicinal components of a single herb, or to increase the potency of a combination.

In addition to herbs, Ayurvedic preparations may contain minerals such as zinc, iron and calcium. Minerals are typically used in remedies to bolster the efficacy of herbs, or to address mineral deficiencies. Some minerals may also be combined into oils, creams and other preparations for topical use.

Many Ayurvedic preparations are prepared using processes such as decoctions, infusions and macerations. These processes involve soaking the herbs in water in order to extract their active components. Decoctions involve boiling the herbs, infusions involve steeping the herbs in hot water, and macerations involve soaking the herbs in cold water or alcohol. Each of these processes is believed to contribute to the medicinal properties of an Ayurvedic preparation.

It is believed that Ayurvedic preparations typically based on herbal compounds can be beneficial for overall health and can address specific health conditions. As with any other medical remedy, it is important to consult a qualified healthcare professional before using an Ayurvedic preparation in order to ensure the safety and efficacy of the remedy.

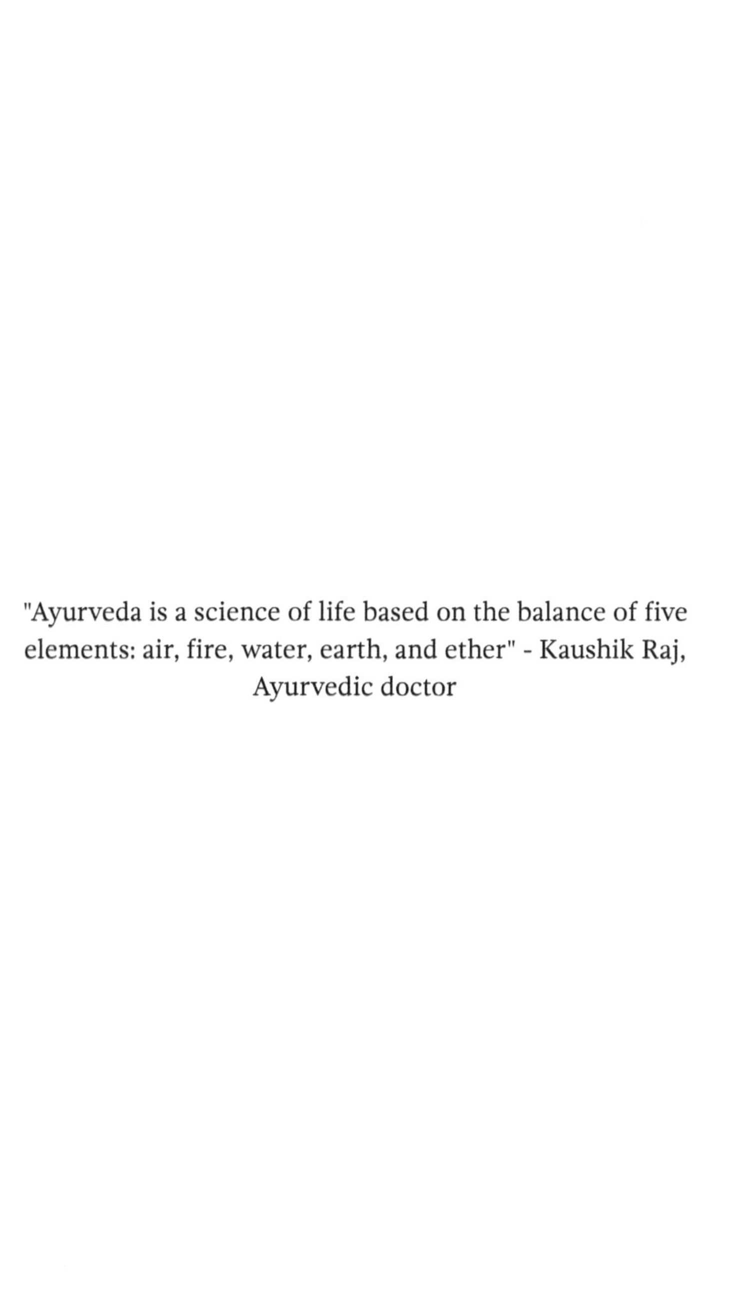

"Ayurveda is a science of life based on the balance of five elements: air, fire, water, earth, and ether" - Kaushik Raj, Ayurvedic doctor

CHAPTER FIVE

ANCIENT INDIAN SCHOLAR OF AYURVEDA

Ayurveda is a system of traditional Indian medicine that has been around since ancient times. The ancient Indian scholars of Ayurveda have shaped the history of this system and have had a lasting impact on its development and usage. These scholars have dedicated their lives to the study of the principles of Ayurveda and have demonstrated both practical and theoretical application of these principles.

The earliest scholar of Ayurveda was Charaka, who is thought to have lived sometime between 1500-1000 BCE. He is credited with creating the 'Charaka Samhita', which is now one of the foundational texts of Ayurvedic medicine. One of Charaka's greatest contributions was the identification of three 'humours' which form the basis of Ayurvedic medicine: Vata (air), Pitta (fire), and Kapha (water). He is also said to have been the first to mark the importance of a holistic approach to treating illness and emphasised the connection between body, mind and soul in achieving health and wellbeing.

Sushruta is the second great scholar of Ayurveda and is famous for writing the 'Sushruta Samhita', which is another foundational text of the discipline. He is credited with the introduction of surgical procedures in Ayurveda and is considered the 'father of surgery' in India. He documented over 200 surgeries and created a classification of medical conditions based on their severity. Additionally, Sushruta is credited with introducing the concept of four levels of doctor-patient relationships and emphasising the importance of medical ethics in treating patients.

The third great scholar of Ayurveda is Vagbhat. He is believed to have lived in around 500 CE and is the author of the 'Ashtanga Hridayam' and the 'Ashtanga Samgraha'. These texts are still used to this day for understanding the principles of Ayurveda. He is said to have been the first to truly understand the connection between the five-element theory and the energy systems of the body. He was also the first to articulate the 'tridosha' concept, which means the idea that all illness is caused by a disruption in the balance of the three humours.

The last great scholar of Ayurveda is Vaghbhat. He was born around 900 CE and is credited with writing the 'Rasayana Chikitsa', which details the use of herbal medicines as a therapeutic tool. He was also the first to describe the concept of Marmacarya, a holistic approach to health and healing focused on balancing the body's energies. He is credited with introducing the concept of 'panchakarma', which is a five-step process used to detoxify and rejuvenate the body.

The four ancient Indian scholars of Ayurveda have made significant contributions to the understanding of this system.

"Ayurveda is about creating harmony between the body, the mind and the environment" - B.S.S. Prasad, Ayurvedic doctor

CHAPTER SIX

SUSHRUTA SAMHITA

Sushruta Samhita is the seventh-century classic of ayurvedic wisdom written by the ancient Indian physician and scholar, Sushruta. The text is composed of six volumes containing hundreds of chapters, each discussing various health topics including physiology, embryology, general principles of healthcare, pathology, diagnosis & treatment, dietary principles and surgical techniques. The text is considered to be the foundation of Indian medicine, so much so that it is often referred to as the 'the mother of Indian medicine.'

Sushruta was a renowned physician and scholar who laid the groundwork for early Indian medical practices. He studied the human body, devising theories about how the body works and the clinical aspects of medical practice. He classified diseases into four broad categories: curable, incurable, treatable and preventable. He is also credited with developing the categorization of ground ingredients, identifying herbs, and devising the different branches of physiology, pathology, hygiene and toxicology.

Sushruta's treatise on medical practices, the Sushruta Samhita, is still revered and considered to be the primary source of ayurvedic knowledge, even over 2,000 years later. The text contains elaborate instructions on many preventative and curative treatments, discussing topics ranging from anatomy and pathology to medication and surgery. This includes methods and instructions related to pre and post-operative care such as the use of herbs, oils and various other medicines.

The approach taken in the text is intended to be holistic. It focuses on the body as an interconnected system, understanding the possible connection between the physical and mental states. This includes understanding the importance of diet, lifestyle, habits, and balanced environment for achieving optimal health. The text further argues for the importance of personalized medical treatment, stating that it is important to analyze the individual's specific conditions and body type before administering any kind of treatment.

Sushruta authored several works on ayurvedic medicine, but the Sushruta Samhita is regarded as the earliest, authentic and most comprehensive ayurvedic treatise available. Although a product of its time, the text still plays an integral role in modern medical practices.

The Sushruta Samhita has been translated in many different languages and is credited with paving the way for modern academic study of traditional medicine in India. The fame of this ancient Indian text has spread far and wide, and today it serves as important text for understanding Indian medical practice. The text is therefore a priceless source of understanding of the relationship between the human body and its environment, representing the cumulative wisdom

of generations of physicians and scholars devoted to the
holistic health and well-being of mankind.

"The wisdom of Ayurveda lies in recognizing and restoring the balance between the body and mind of the individual" - Agastya, ancient Indian scholar

CHAPTER SEVEN

CHARAKA SAMHITA

Charaka, one of the most influential scholars of ayurveda, is remembered for his contribution to the Indian medicinal system. His book Charaka Samhita, written in approximately 400 BC, is highly recognized within the scientific and medical fields as a remarkable literary work. Charaka is seen as a great teacher, healer and unprecedented researcher of the ayurvedic tradition. In the Charaka Samhita, he presents a vivid overview of the traditional Indian view of health, illness, anatomy, and the medicinal uses of plants and herbs.

It is believed that Charaka originated from the Sakadvipa region near present-day Nepal. Although it is uncertain whether he was a student of another teacher or if he founded his own school of thought, there is no doubt that his contribution to the ayurvedic system had a great impact on the development of modern medicine. He was a respected physician who provided treatments to numerous prominent individuals, including the Mauryan emperor, Ashoka.

In Charaka Samhita, Charaka presents his ideas on various topics, particularly those relating to the preservation of health and curing disease. For example, he argued that illnesses are caused by imbalances in the three bodily humours (vata, pitta and kapha) and that their balances in the body must be restored in order to restore health. He also proposed that health depended on a good diet, proper sleep, relaxation and good relationships with others, as well as other spiritual and mental practices. This provides an insight into the holistic view of health that he proposed.

Charaka also views plants and herbs as major contributors to healing and health. In the Charaka Samhita, he describes various herbal medicines and their use in healing various conditions. He also stresses the importance of particular environments and climates for the cultivation of certain plants and herbs. Charaka's research is known to be one of the earliest forms of pharmacology.

In addition, Charaka explains the use of diet, lifestyle and the connection between mind and body in ayurveda. His book delves into the relationships between the body, environment and mind-body unity. He suggests that the environment and its elements contribute to the humours of the body and, consequently, its health. He also suggests ways to tame the mind, such as rituals, yoga and physical exercises.

In conclusion, Charaka is an important figure in the history of ayurveda and modern medicine. His book Charaka Samhita provides a valuable insight into traditional Indian medicinal knowledge and continues to have a profound influence on the development of modern medicine. His contributions to understanding the relationship between the body, environment and the mind-body unity have had a lasting effect on our understanding of health.

"Ayurveda enables us to see health holistically, rather than as something to be treated superficially, as a set of symptoms" - Dhanvantari, ancient Indian physician

CHAPTER EIGHT

VAGHBHAT

Vaghbhat, or Charaka Vaghbhat, was one of the earliest scholars of the Ayurveda system of health and well-being. He is believed to have lived in India in the 2nd Century BC. Vaghbhat's works laid a solid foundation for the practice of Ayurveda. In essence, his contribution to the science of Ayurveda could be regarded as one of the hallmarks of Indian knowledge systems.

Vaghbhat is believed to have gathered extensive information from the ancient Vedas and Upanishads, which laid the foundation for his own works. His five treatises, Charaka Samhita (Manual of Charaka), Sushruta Samhita (Treatise of Sushruta), Yogaratnakara (Ocean of Yogic Knowledge), Brihat Trayi (Three Grand Books) and Chikitsasara (Manual for Treatment) are considered landmarks of Ayurvedic knowledge.

Vaghbhat laid great emphasis on the integration of basic ingredients into a single therapeutic protocol according to the specific needs of a patient. He also emphasized the priority of preventing illness by taking into account different factors such as diet and lifestyle. In his Charaka Samhita, he described the three bodily humours (vastu), which are now known as the tridosha in Ayurveda (the three humours of wind, bile, and phlegm), that govern the body's equilibrium. His works also detailed the eight branches of traditional Ayurveda, which are now known as Ashtanga Ayurveda (eight methods or approaches). In addition, he wrote extensively on yoga, the importance of meditation and breathing techniques.

Vaghbhat's contributions to Ayurveda are priceless. His works have become the cornerstone of Ayurvedic treatment, and they have maintained their validity over time. His works have been extensively studied and have heavily influenced modern-day Ayurveda practices, as well as the medical systems that are followed in South East Asia and other regions.

The impact of Vaghbhat's work can be seen in the fact that the practice of Ayurveda is still prevalent in India and is slowly gaining popularity in the Western world as an holistic health care system. Often credited as the father of Ayurveda, Vaghbhat is an example of the many unsung pioneers of Indian knowledge systems and an inspiration to many aspiring Ayurvedic scholars of the present day.

"Ayurveda is the ideal approach to life and health not just because it helps balance the mind, body and spirit, but also because Ayurvedic lifestyle offers ways to lead a healthier, more enriched life" - Deepak Chopra, Ayurveda practitioner

CHAPTER NINE

TRIDOSH

VATA (AIR), PITTA (FIRE), AND KAPHA (WATER)

Ayurveda is an ancient Indian health system that attempts to bring balance to the body and maintain a state of perfect health. One of the most well-known and fundamental principles of Ayurveda is the three different energies, or doshas: Vata (air), Pitta (fire), and Kapha (water).

Vata is the energy of movement, creativity, and fluctuation. It is associated with the wind and governs the movement of blood, energy, and the nervous system. Vata is the source of creativity and imagination and is expressed through bodily processes such as breathing, elimination, and metabolism. Imbalances in Vata can lead to issues with anxiety, digestion, and fatigue. To restore balance to Vata, lifestyle and dietary measures are essential. Ayurveda recommends key practices such as maintaining regular eating habits, avoiding extreme temperatures and hot spices, and going to sleep before 10 PM. Exercise, massage, and mindful practices can also aid in restoring balance.

The next dosha is Pitta, the energy of transformation, digestion, and intense emotions. It is associated with fire and governs the digestion of food and emotions, as well as body temperature, skin complexion, and metabolism. When out of balance, Pitta can cause irritability, inflammation, and excessive heat in the body. To bring balance to Pitta, dietary adjustments such as avoiding hot, spicy foods and reducing your intake of caffeine are recommended. A lifestyle focus that balances activity with rest, and mental practices such as Yoga and meditation can help in restoring a Pitta imbalance.

Finally, Kapha is the energy of stability and structure. It is associated with water and governs the flow of fluid within the body, as well as the lubrication of joints and muscles. Imbalances in Kapha can result in congestion, overweight, and sinus issues. Ayurvedic principles recommend lifestyle adjustments that keep Kapha in balance. Eating lighter and warmer meals and having regular exercise is key, along with reducing the intake of fatty, starchy and sugary foods.

In conclusion, the three doshas of Vata (air), Pitta (fire), and Kapha (water) are key concepts in the practice of Ayurveda, an ancient Indian health system. Each dosha has its own set of characteristics and symptoms when in balance or out of balance. To keep the doshas in balance, dietary and lifestyle adjustments can be made. It is essential to live in harmony with these ancient energies to ensure optimal health and wellbeing.

"Ayurveda is an ancient form of medicine that focuses on the healing power of nature. Ayurvedic remedies are based on the body's constitution, health and environment" - B.K.S. Iyengar, yoga authority

PANCHA KARMA

Ayurveda, an ancient medical martial developed in India, is one of the oldest form of healing known. It uses a holistic approach to treating the mind and body by using natural substances such as plants, herbs, and minerals. One of the most important aspects of Ayurvedic healing is Panchakarma, a cleansing practice that helps rid the body of toxins and brings balance to the three doshas, or energy systems.

Panchakarma is a Sanskrit word that translates to "five therapies." It is composed of five separate parts, each of which works together to detoxify and restore balance to the body. The five components of Panchakarma are: Vamana (vomiting), Virechana (purging), Nasya (nasal cleansing), Basti (enema) and Rakta Mokshana (bloodletting).

Vamana is the practice of inducing vomiting in order to remove toxins from the digestive system. The patient is given a herbal preparation to drink and then monitored carefully to ensure that the correct level of vomiting is achieved. This can take anywhere from fifteen minutes to two hours, although most people need only a few minutes to be cured.

Virechana is a special purgation technique used to remove toxins from the body. It involves consuming a laxative or purgative that is carefully prepared according to Ayurvedic principles. The patient is monitored to ensure that the toxins are expelled from the body. This is often done in combination with Vamana, as the purpose of both Vamana and Virechana is to eliminate toxins from the body.

Nasya therapy is a form of nasal cleansing that helps to clear the respiratory passages of mucus and other toxins. A combination of herbal oils, ghee (clarified butter), and herbs is administered through the nostrils. This helps to lubricate and soothe the nasal passages while also removing toxins.

Basti is an Ayurvedic speciality in which substances such as oils and herbs are administered into the intestine through the rectum. This helps to flush out toxins and mucus from the large intestine. This is often done in conjunction with Virechana, as both treatments work to remove toxins from the body.

Rakta Mokshana is the practice of removing toxins from the body by means of bloodletting. This can be done with medicinal herbs and other substances, as well as through leeches or razor blades. Since this method can be dangerous and has potential side effects, it should only be done under the supervision of a trained Ayurvedic practitioner.

Panchakarma is an important component of Ayurvedic medicine and should be used in conjunction with other treatments, such as herb-based remedies, to achieve optimal results.

Ayurveda offers challenges and insights to the wise western scientist and physician."—Joseph E. Pizzorno Jr., prominent naturopathic doctor and scientist.

CHAPTER ELEVEN

FAMOUS TEXTS ON AYURVEDA

Ayurveda is one of the oldest systems of healing in the world, having arisen in India over 5,000 years ago. It is still widely practiced today, and many Indian communities rely on Ayurveda for their general healthcare. Because of its history and historical significance in Indian society, many famous texts have been written about Ayurveda.

The most famous Ayurvedic texts are the Charaka Samhita, the Sushruta Samhita, and the Bhavaprakasha. The Charaka Samhita, which is probably the oldest of these texts, was believed to have been written in the 1st or 2nd century BC by an ancient sage. It is a comprehensive medical textbook that covers numerous aspects of health and disease, including anatomy, physiology, pathology, treatment, and prognosis. It is still highly influential in modern Ayurvedic practice today.

The Sushruta Samhita, written by the sage Sushruta, is a compendium of six books. These books cover topics ranging from anatomy and physiology to surgery, dentistry, and healthcare for children. It is considered one of the main sources of Ayurvedic knowledge and still serves as a fundamental reference text for practitioners.

The Bhavaprakasha is a more recent text, written by Bhavamisra in the 16th century. This text provides information on Ayurvedic principles and practices, including anatomy, physiology, pharmacology, diet and lifestyle, pathology, and therapeutic interventions. It is highly influential in modern Ayurvedic medicine and is at the heart of most contemporary approaches to Ayurveda.

In addition to the Charaka Samhita, the Sushruta Samhita, and the Bhavaprakasha, there are numerous other important Ayurvedic texts. One of the most important of these is the Ashtanga Hrdayam, which was compiled by the renowned Ayurvedic physician Vaghbata in the 6th century. This text covers the fundamentals of Ayurveda, including anatomy, physiology, diagnosis, and treatments.

The Ayurvedic texts have had a profound influence not just on the science and practice of Ayurveda, but on Indian culture and society as a whole. These texts are still widely read and consulted as reference works for practitioners to this day. They are also a source of knowledge for students of Ayurveda and others who are interested in the history and culture of India and Ayurveda. As such, they continue to be an integral part of the Indian cultural and intellectual heritage.

Ayurveda has withstood the test of time to become the oldest continually practiced medical system in the world. Ayurveda's holistic approach to health and well-being is as relevant today as it was over 5,000 years ago."—Dr. Deepak Chopra, holistic healer and spiritual guru.

CHAPTER TWELVE

MODERN APPROACH TO AYURVEDA AROUND THE WORLD

Ayurveda is an ancient healing system from India considered the world's oldest health science, predating both Chinese and Western medical systems. It includes various forms of traditional medicine, including yoga, meditation and massage, and is still widely practiced today. Ayurveda is based on the belief that by nurturing and balancing the mind, body and spirit, a person can achieve optimal health. The ancient Ayurvedic knowledge is still largely relevant in the modern world, and its concepts have become increasingly popular both in India and around the world.

Recently, there has been a significant shift in the way Ayurveda is viewed and used around the world. In the past, most of the knowledge was restricted to India and was not widely known or utilized. However, due to growing interest, more people are looking to Ayurveda for general health and wellness, and practitioners of Ayurveda can be found in clinics, spas, and health centers around the world.

The modern approach to Ayurveda puts greater emphasis on understanding and managing the root cause of ill health. Instead of looking solely at individual symptoms, practitioners look at the entire person and seek to provide a balanced and holistic approach to healing. This approach is based on one's individual constitution (known as 'prakriti' in Ayurveda), which is determined by examining one's lifestyle, habits and environment. The goal of this approach is to bring balance and harmony to the body's elemental energies.

Traditional Ayurvedic treatments such as herbs, oils, massage therapies, lifestyle advice and nutritional guidance are still the foundation of modern Ayurvedic practice. However, the modern approach to Ayurveda often includes the integration of modern science and Western medicine in order to better understand and address a person's health issues (such as chronic conditions and stress-related moments). For example, Ayurvedic practitioners might use modern diagnostics and laboratory tests to get a better understanding of a patient's health.

Additionally, modern Ayurvedic practice has increasingly embraced technology, and many practitioners now offer consultations and treatments over Skype, making them more accessible to people around the world. Digital tools have also made it easier to access reliable Ayurvedic information and treatments.

Overall, the modern approach to Ayurveda has helped to make this ancient practice more accessible and mainstream. As the popularity of Ayurveda continues to grow, many Western doctors are now recognizing its potential to complement traditional medical approaches, leading to a better understanding and greater acceptance of this holistic health system.

"Ayurveda is one of the oldest sciences of healing on the planet. Its principles have been used to treat many physical and mental illnesses successfully for centuries."—Dr. Andrew Weil, pioneer in holistic medicine.

AYURVEDA IN EUROPE

The ancient Indian system of medicine, known as Ayurveda and its therapeutic practices, have been gaining more and more popularity in Europe lately. This traditional science of life has a holistic approach, aimed at promotion of health, prevention of diseases and finally, increasing the longevity of life. It revolves around the principles of balance, harmony, knowledge and balance between mind, body and spirit.

Ayurveda stands out of traditional medicine as it uses herbs and other natural ingredients to treat both physical and psychological ailments. The five major aspects of Ayurveda focus on areas such as lifestyle, nutrition, detoxification and rejuvenation and treatment. These areas are inter-related, requiring a focus on personal self-care and regular health maintenance.

The popularity of Ayurvedic medicine in Europe can be partly attributed to the holistic, natural approach which is in contrast with a lot of the more aggressive and obtrusive treatments used in conventional medicine. Massage and yoga are widely used to relax the body and mind and to help the body heal naturally and effectively. The concept of balance and harmony that the Ayurveda promotes has also contributed to its popularity, as it helps people become conscious of how their lifestyle and nutrition may be affecting their health.

Furthermore, good health is usually considered to be synonymous with good beauty and people want to look good, thus they turn to Ayurveda in order to help them achieve and maintain a healthy, beautiful appearance. From herbs like amla to beauty regimes like the oil baths, Ayurveda provides a gentle yet effective way to enhance one's beauty and presence, both inside and out.

Ayurvedic medicines, when taken with guidance from a qualified Ayurveda practitioner, are known to be quite safe, with minimal risk of side effects. In fact, the therapeutic potential of Ayurvedic services is increasingly being recognized and embraced by European medical systems due to its integrated approach and natural treatments.

The popularity of Ayurveda in Europe reflects the changing attitude towards health and well being, where more people are looking for natural, gentle methods to maintain their health and beauty. Ayurvedic treatments provide a modality that is much less intrusive than conventional treatments, while still providing positive benefits. As more people turn to Ayurveda, its influence in Europe is sure to expand, impacting a growing population of those looking to live a balanced life rooted in natural healing.

It is extraordinary that a system of medicine this ancient
still provides the basis of much of twentieth century
knowledge in human physiology, pathology,
pharmacology and diet."—Sir John H. Whitaker, noted
British doctor and scholar.

AYURVEDA IN AMERICAN COUNTRIES

Ayurveda is an ancient system of traditional healing that originated in India over fifteen centuries ago. Ayurvedic medicine and treatments have become increasingly popular in the United States and other Western countries in recent years, due in part to the greater availability of credible information about the science and effects of ayurvedic medicine.

Ayurveda is founded on the idea of tailoring a plan to the individual person rather than a one-size-fits-all approach to health care. According to ayurvedic principles, maintaining good health requires balancing each individual's unique physical, emotional, and mental constitution. To achieve this holistic balance, ayurvedic treatments range from simple lifestyle modifications and home remedies to diet and yoga to more complex therapies like herbal remedies and massage.

One of the main attractions to Ayurveda in America is its emphasis on using natural, non-toxic treatments. Ayurvedic treatments are based on the concept that the body has an inner intelligence and that, given the proper diet, exercise, relaxation techniques, and herbal medicines, it will naturally bring itself into balance. Research studies have also linked ayurvedic practices to better brain function, cognitive benefits, and increased immunity to stress.

Additionally, ayurveda is growing increasingly popular due to its holistic approach and its emphasis on the mind-body connection. The science of ayurveda holds that it is possible to achieve health and balance in all aspects of life by using ayurvedic medicines and treatments. Rather than exclusively targeting physical symptoms of illness, ayurveda seeks to address all areas of wellbeing: physical, mental, spiritual, and emotional.

Overall, it's clear that ayurveda and ayurvedic medicine have gained a foothold in American culture. This system of healing is becoming increasingly popular and respected due to its holistic approach to health, its emphasis on natural treatments, and its non-invasive, individualized approach to healthcare. As more and more research confirms ayurvedic principles, this system of healing is likely to become even more popular and accepted in the United States.

"Ayurveda is a complete medical system with a rich mythology, elegant theory and effective clinical tools. Ayurveda provides a system of self-care that is appropriate for all individuals."—Larissa Hall Carlson, Ayurvedic practitioner and author.

CHAPTER FIFTEEN

NAGARJUNA'S WORKS ON AYURVED

Nagarjuna is one of the most important figures of the early development of Indian Buddhist philosophy. He is known for his influential works on Madhyamaka (middle path), which provides a profound philosophical system of analysis and reflection on Buddhist doctrine. Not only did he provide the framework for Madhyamaka Buddhist analysis, but he also drew upon and extended upon previous Indian philosophical and theological debates. His writings have had a huge impact on subsequent philosophical and religious thinkers, both in India and abroad.

One of the most important aspects of Nagarjuna's philosophical views was his articulation of the Madhyamaka middle path. This was an effort to identify the basic Buddhist tenets of emptiness, suffering and liberation, and to create a system for understanding them in a deeply philosophical manner. Nagarjuna's Madhyamaka teachings affirmed the two truths doctrine, which taught that there are both conventional and ultimate realities. Contrary to the approach of early Buddhist thinking, Nagarjuna suggested that ultimate reality is beyond understanding, which left people open to living inbetween and reconciling both conventional and ultimate truths.

In addition to Nagarjuna's works on Madhyamaka, his medical works on Ayurveda played a major role in the development and preservation of this ancient system of medicine. Ayurveda is defined as a science of life and has been used to treat physical, mental and spiritual ailments. Nagarjuna's works provided an early analysis of the principles of Ayurveda, including nutrition, diagnosis and treatment of diseases. His theories on herbal medicines, dietary intake and cleansing practices had a lasting impact on the development and practice of Ayurvedic medicine.

All in all, Nagarjuna's works had a major impact on early Indian philosophy, as well as on Buddhist thought. His works on Madhyamaka represent a major contribution to philosophical debate, while his medical works on Ayurveda provided a robust system for the practice of the system for generations. Each of these works have had lasting consequence, making Nagarjuna truly one of India's most important intellectual figures and thinkers.

"Ayurveda is an example of man-made science utilized centuries before modern Western medicine was developed. Ayurvedic treatments are personalized and based on the belief that an individual's physical, mental, and spiritual health must be balanced."—Christopher M. Columbus, writer and public health advocate.

EIGHT WAYS OF AYURVEDA TO DIAGNOSE ILLNESS

Ayurveda is an ancient system of traditional Indian medicine that is based on restoring balance and wellness in the body. This system of holistic healing includes treatments such as herbal remedies, massage and meditation. Ayurveda emphasizes preventative measures rather than alleviating symptoms, which makes it particularly well-suited to diagnosing illnesses. Ayurveda has eight different methods for diagnosing illnesses, all of which can be used together to form a comprehensive picture of the health of the patient.

The first way to diagnose illness according to Ayurveda is through observing body language and other clues. By watching the patient's facial expressions, posture, breathing, gait and manner of speaking, the practitioner can learn a great deal about the person's physical and mental wellbeing. They may also look for more subtle clues such as the color of the person's skin or the texture of their hair, and take detailed notes of the overall impression of their health.

The second way is palpation, or feeling the pulse. Measuring the pulse rate gives the practitioner a great deal of information about the patient's state of health. Changes in pulse rate can signal different stages of illness, and can be tracked to identify any changes in the patient's health. Additionally, the temperature of the pulse can reveal a great deal about the status of both the patient's physical and mental wellbeing.

The third method of diagnosis used in Ayurveda is examining the tongue. The tongue can reveal a great deal about the health of the patient, from subtle changes in color and texture to more obvious inflammation and sores. Additionally, the size and shape of the tongue can indicate various illnesses, with a swollen and inflamed tongue often being a sign of infection or illness.

The fourth method used in Ayurveda is taking a detailed history of the patient's illness. This includes learning about the patient's current condition as well as past medical problems and any family history of chronic illnesses. This allows the practitioner to identify any predisposition to particular ailments, and can also provide insight into any environmental or lifestyle factors that may have contributed to the illness.

The fifth method used by Ayurveda practitioners is examining the patient's eyes. A detailed examination of the pupils, iris and cornea can reveal important information about the functioning of the body. Changes in the way the eyes respond to light, the color of the iris, and the amount of moisture the eyes produce can all be taken into consideration when diagnosing illness.

Ayurveda, the ancient Hindu science of healing, is a holistic approach to wellness through the use of proper diet, lifestyle, and herbs. One of the primary tools employed in Ayurveda for understanding an individual's health is called "Nadi Vijnana" or pulse diagnosis.

Nadi Vijnana is used to assess the various organs and systems of the body in order to diagnose illness and prescribe treatments. This form of pulse diagnosis is broken down into eight distinct stages. These stages are known as the sixth, seventh and eighth ways of the Ayurvedic system.

The sixth way of diagnoses uses examination of the heart rate. By feeling the radial arteries, the practitioner can detect the subtle variations in the speed and strength of the heart beat. This can offer insights into the health of the various organs and tissues of the body and indicate any obstructions to the cardiovascular system.

The seventh way of diagnosis involves looking for irregularities in the color, texture or consistency of the pulse. The practitioner looks at the color, appearance and quality of the pulse to deduce the health of the digestive and respiratory systems.

The eighth and final way of diagnosis involves feeling the veins in the wrists and neck area. This method is used to observe the quality of blood circulation in the body and examine issues related to the kidneys, urinary system and blood pressure. Additionally, the practitioner will look for indications of organ damage and toxins, as well as evidence of nutrient deficiencies.

By combining the various stages of pulse diagnosis, the Ayurvedic practitioner can accurately assess and diagnose any underlying illness in an individual. Through this comprehensive system, the practitioner can identify the root cause of any physical, mental or emotional imbalance. The eight diagnostic techniques outlined by Ayurveda are an effective tool for understanding health on a holistic level

Ayurveda also employs urine tests, fecal tests, X-rays and breath analysis to diagnose illnesses. Urine tests can provide information about general health, as well as metabolic and kidney function.

"Ayurveda is of particular value due to its focus on maintaining wellbeing by understanding and addressing the causal factors of ill health."—Dr. Peter Fisher, Royal London Hospital's Director of Research and Professor of Complementary Medicine.

CHAPTER SEVENTEEN

TULSI-FLOWER (HOLY BASIL), AN AYURVEDIC HERB

Tulsi-flower, also known as holy basil, is an Ayurvedic herb that has been used for centuries across India and Southeast Asia for its medicinal and spiritual properties. Its botanical name is Ocimum sanctum; it is a herbal plant from the Lamiaceae family, closely related to culinary basil.

Tulsi is considered an important herb in the Ayurvedic practice and the Hindu religion, and its health benefits and spiritual properties are chronicled in ancient Sanskrit texts. Tulsi is believed to be an earthly manifestation of the goddess Tulsi Devi, often referred to as "the incomparable one." Hindus revere the Tulsi-flower and many Indian households have a Tulsi plant growing in their yards or in pots on their balconies.

Tulsi is considered a healing plant with numerous medicinal benefits. In India, it is commonly referred to as "the elixir of life" because it is known to treat a variety of conditions, from common colds and flus, to inflammation, asthma, diabetes, and liver and kidney diseases. It has anti-stress and anti-inflammatory properties, and it can help boost immunity and reduce anxiety, headaches, and fever. Tulsi has anti-bacterial, anti-fungal, and anti-viral properties and can help with digestion, mental health, and skin issues.

Tulsi is said to possess natural detoxifying properties and it is often used in herbal teas and with food. As a component of traditional Ayurvedic medicine, the herb is often used to treat a variety of conditions. It can be consumed in a variety of forms—dried, powdered, mixed in pastes, and grinded into the form of oil.

From a spiritual perspective, Tulsi is believed to purify the soul and provide strength to a person's spirit. It is often used as an offering to gods and goddesses in Hindu rituals, and is said to bring happiness and good luck to those who revere and offer it prayerfully. By simply growing the Tulsi-flower nearby and offering prayers to it daily, Hindus believe they will gain spiritual benefits and be guided on the right path.

In summary, Tulsi-flower is an Ayurvedic herb with a long history of medicinal use and spiritual symbolism. It has long been revered in India and Southeast Asia for its therapeutic benefits and spiritual symbolism. It can be used to make herbal tea, with food, as a component of traditional Ayurvedic medicines, and as an offering to gods in Hindu rituals.

"Ayurveda is especially suited to the modern world as it offers an holistic view of health, taking into account a person's environment, lifestyle, and nutrition."—Dr. Robert Svoboda, ayurvedic physician and author.

CHAPTER EIGHTEEN

AYURVEDA IN INDIA, BANGLADESH, SRI LANKA

Ayurveda is an ancient and traditional medical system that originated in India about 5000 years ago. It is a Sanskrit word which stands for knowledge of life (Ayu = life; Veda = knowledge). The Ayurvedic approach to disease is based on the belief that the body is made up of five fundamental elements (Earth, Water, Fire, Air and Ether) and three life forces known as doshas. The three doshas are Vata, Pitta, and Kapha and they help to maintain balance in the body. The practice of Ayurveda is a holistic approach which emphasizes prevention and the use of natural remedies to treat and cure diseases.

Ayurveda has been an integral part of Indian culture for centuries, but it has gained increasing acceptance in other countries in the past few decades. Today, Ayurveda is widely practiced in many countries like India, Bangladesh, and Sri Lanka. In Sri Lanka, Ayurveda is largely used as a complementary form of health care, providing natural treatments that are both safe and effective. In Bangladesh, Ayurveda is gaining in popularity due to the stress relief and relaxation benefits associated with it. In India, Ayurveda is a holistic form of medicine and has become a part of everyday life.

The main focus of Ayurveda is prevention of disease, through diet and lifestyle changes. An Ayurvedic physician will look at a person's constitution, diet and lifestyle and make recommendations for how to maintain health. According to the principles of Ayurveda, diseases are caused by imbalances in the body, and these imbalances can be corrected through diet, lifestyle changes and the use of herbal remedies.

Ayurveda focuses on the use of naturally occurring substances such as herbal remedies, teas, oils and spices to treat diseases. Herbal medicines are used to treat a variety of ailments such as colds, flu, headaches, digestive disorders, skin problems and joint pain. In addition to herbal medicines, Ayurveda employs a variety of other treatments, such as massage therapies, yoga, pranayama, meditation and various breathing exercises.

In conclusion, Ayurveda is a holistic approach to health and well-being that is based on the principles of balance and prevention. It is widely used in countries such as India, Bangladesh and Sri Lanka, and is becoming increasingly popular in Western countries as well. By following an Ayurvedic lifestyle, one can improve their overall health, reduce their risk of illness, and lead a happier and healthier life.

"Ayurveda holds the secret to a vital system that most of us were unacquainted with—until now."—Dr. Robert H. Reeb, yoga and Ayurveda

CHAPTER NINETEEN

MODERN APPROACH TO AYURVEDA

Ayurveda is an ancient form of medicine and healing that originated in India more than 5,000 years ago. This holistic system of healing looks beyond the physical symptoms and seeks to identify the underlying cause of illness by using a variety of diagnostic tools such as pulse reading, iridology, and tongue diagnosis. The goal is to help the patient find balance in their life and mind to prevent and treat conditions.

Nowadays, modern practitioners of Ayurveda have adapted the ancient practice to meet the needs of contemporary society. The traditional methods are still used to diagnose and treat illnesses and to restore balance, but modern practitioners have incorporated new approaches and technologies to provide more effective treatments.

For example, Ayurveda treats the body holistically with botanical medicines, massage therapy, yoga, and dietary and lifestyle modifications to help restore proper balance. The use of modern technologies such as ultrasonography and EEG has helped practitioners to identify and treat sources of imbalance more quickly and accurately.

Ayurveda also emphasizes the importance of preventive care to stay healthy and balanced. For example, the practice suggests that changes in lifestyle such as getting adequate sleep, eating balanced meals, and avoiding toxins can help maintain physical and emotional wellbeing. It also teaches techniques to manage stress levels through meditation, yoga, and breathing exercises.

In addition to modern technologies and preventive care, modern practitioners of Ayurveda are now offering treatments tailored to the individual's specific needs. This approach takes into account the patient's individual physiology, environment, lifestyle, and mental state to devise a custom treatment plan.

The rise of the internet has also made Ayurveda more accessible, allowing people to find practitioners and educational resources more easily. Additionally, many practitioners are now providing telehealth consultations, allowing more people to access these treatments from the comfort of their own homes.

Modern ayurvedic practices have adapted traditional treatments to provide more effective and personalized services for modern patients. This has led to an increase in the popularity of Ayurveda with many people recognizing its benefits for helping maintain physical and mental wellbeing in a holistic way.

"Ayurveda is an effective medicine, prevention and therapy all in one" - Dr. Vasant Lad, Ayurvedic Doctor

CHAPTER TWENTY

NEW ERA SCHOLARS AND THEIR WORK ON AYURVEDA

The study of Ayurveda, an ancient Indian system of natural healing, is a subject both revered and respected around the world. Over the centuries, numerous great scholars have dedicated their lives to this field, pushing its boundaries and making contributions to its evolution. This essay will discuss some of the most influential researchers in Ayurveda, beginning in the early 20th century, who have left a lasting impact on the field.

The first scholar of note is P. Shanmugasundaram, or Papa Sundaram who, in the early 1900s, began research on Ayurveda and its medicinal properties. His ground-breaking work on toxicity and toxicity tests played a large role in pushing the development of modern Ayurveda. Later, his colleague, Dr. Vaidya V.Telang oversaw the standardization of Ayurvedic medicines through the 'Ayurveda Bio standardized formulas', a huge milestone in traditional medicine.

In the 1950s and 60s, Prof. K.R. Srikanthan from the Banaras Hindu University worked tirelessly to popularize Ayurveda among the general population and worked to create a better understanding of the field for modern scholarship. One of Srikanthan's contributions was the first book on Ayurveda, entitled 'Ayurveda Sourabha', an encyclopedia of Ayurvedic knowledge and information. His extensive research resulted in the publication of two text books on the subject, 'Ayurvedic Practices' and 'Ayurveda Samhita.'

In the later part of the 20th century, Dr. Satyanath Sarkar, who was part of the Central Council for Research in Ayurveda (CCRAS), pushed research on Ayurvedic medicine and its application for treating various diseases. His work and discoveries connecting the planets to the human body and health, known as 'planetary Ayurveda,' served as a foundation for the future of Ayurvedic research.

Dr. Pushkar Dwivedi is another key researcher ofAyurveda, who served as director of CCRAS, Institute of Postgraduate Teaching and Research in Ayurveda, Gujarat. During his tenure, he established and developed an overall system for producing standardized Ayurvedic medicines and developed programs to properly train and educate medical professionals in the field of Ayurveda. This allowed for larger scale applications and understanding of Ayurvedic treatment.

Today, many professors and scholars continue to build on the legacy of these incredible individuals. Their contributions to Ayurveda have proven invaluable to the field and have enabled it to become widely accepted and studied around the world. As modern day scholars look to find solutions to various ailments, their findings will further develop Ayurveda and ensure its progress for generations to come.

CHAPTER TWENTY-ONE

AYURVEDA IN MIDDLE EAST COUNTRIES

Ayurveda, an ancient form of traditional medicine commonly practiced in India, is slowly gaining traction in the Middle East. This trend is undoubtedly driven by the region's strong historical ties with India and the increasingly high interest in alternative and holistic approaches to health.

Ayurveda is an ancient practice of medicine founded on the natural components of the body and the environment. It seeks to understand the cause of an ailment and provide healing by treating the natural balance of the body. This approach often includes diet and lifestyle changes, herbs, yoga, and other forms of massage therapy. Ayurveda also claims to treat imbalances in the mind and recognizes the importance of psychological balance to overall health and wellness.

In recent years, there has been an increasing awareness of Ayurveda in the Middle East region. People are now embracing its holistic principles in their daily health practices and treatments. This is especially true in the larger cities such as Dubai, Abu Dhabi, and Riyadh, where institutions such as the Ayurvedic and Oriental Medicine College of Dubai are providing treatments in both traditional and modern practices.

The region is showing a special interest in its application in promoting healthy living through diet and lifestyle. People are increasingly following a diet plan catering to the principles of Ayurveda such as increased whole grains and fresh vegetables, with an emphasis on seasonal produce. This trend can be seen in the increasing popularity of Ayurvedic menus in the cities' restaurants.

Traditional treatments such as oil massages and abhyangam are being increasingly sought-after in the region. Herbal therapies and ayurvedic medicines are also being explored for a variety of maladies ranging from disabilities to chronic fatigue. This is part of a larger trend of holistic medicine being embraced as part of an effort to restore the mind and body back to a harmonious state.

Overall, Ayurveda is becoming increasingly popular in Tunisia, Saudi Arabia, the UAE, and other places in the Middle East. People are becoming more educated on the benefits of Ayurveda in their overall health, and the demand for its treatments is expected to rise significantly. This trend is expected to boost the market share of the ayurvedic sector in the upcoming years, making the practice even more famous.

CHAPTER TWENTY-TWO

FAMOUS AYURVEDIC MEDICINAL PLANTS

Ayurveda is a form of traditional Indian medicine that is based on ancient Vedic scripture. Traditional Ayurvedic medicinal plants have long been used to treat various medical conditions, from infectious diseases to chronic illnesses. While India may be the birthplace of Ayurveda, the practice of Ayurvedic medicine has spread to many parts of the world and become popular in the West.

Tulsi or holy basil is one of the most widely recognized and utilized Ayurvedic medicinal plants. This sacred plant has been used as a medicinal plant in India for centuries. Tulsi is known to treat respiratory conditions, improve digestion, reduce fever, and boost immunity. It is also believed to help soothe the mind and body. This versatile herb can be taken in several forms including tinctures, infusions, and oils.

Ashwagandha is another invaluable Ayurvedic medicinal plant. This plant is commonly used to boost energy levels and for its adaptogen properties. It is believed to fight anxiety and stress, enhance memory and concentration, and improve overall immune system health. It can also be used to reduce inflammation and improve mood. It can be consumed as a beverage or taken in capsule form.

Amalaki is a shrub-like ayurvedic plant that is used as a medicinal agent for a variety of conditions. This fruit is known as a natural source of vitamin C, and it is often used to reduce cholesterol and boost energy levels. It is also used to support digestion and detoxification. In addition, Amalaki is known to be a powerful antioxidant and is believed to reduce the risk of developing cancer and other inflammatory conditions. It can be taken as an herbal supplement or included in various food preparations.

Haritaki is another potent Ayurvedic medicinal plant. This ayurvedic fruit is used to treat respiratory ailments, indigestion, inflammation, and even skin conditions such as acne. It is believed to promote longevity and is often taken to reduce fatigue and improve mental clarity. Haritaki is also known to have anti-parasitic properties, and can be taken as capsules, extracts, or pastes.

These are only a few of the numerous Ayurvedic medicinal plants that have been used for centuries to promote health and wellbeing. With their powerful medicinal properties and diverse healing abilities, these medicinal plants provide a valuable source of natural healing. As with any form of medicine, it is important to consult a qualified practitioner before beginning any treatment or supplementing with any of these plants.

CHAPTER TWENTY-THREE

FOOD AND EATING RESTRICTIONS IN AYURVEDA

Ayurveda is an ancient medical system of India that dates back 5,000 years. It is based on the premise that health and wellness depend on a balance between the mind, body, and spirit. It uses a holistic approach to health and wellbeing, considering both internal and external factors, including diet. Foods and eating schedules have been carefully studied by Ayurvedic practitioners over the years and support has been provided for the belief that certain eating restrictions, and an appropriate eating schedule, are essential to maintaining health.

Foods are grouped into six main categories in Ayurveda: sweet, sour, salty, pungent, bitter, and astringent. Depending on the type of dosha (constitution) one has, certain foods that should and should not be eaten are prescribed because their quantity, quality and combinations are said to be linked to health. For example, if one has a Vata dosha, high sour and salt foods should be avoided, as it can speed up Vata in the body, contributing to anxiety and insomnia. Likewise, a Pitta dosha person should avoid foods that are hot, spicy and pungent such as chili and garlic, and should instead opt for foods that are cooling, such as cucumbers, apples, and nuts.

Moreover, Ayurveda puts great emphasis on the time of day when eating should occur. Feasting and over-eating should be avoided and instead eating just enough to satisfy hunger should be the priority. Eating should take place preferably between 8AM - 12PM, 2PM – 6PM, and 8PM - 10PM. All meals should be enjoyed in a peaceful and relaxed atmosphere as it is said to enhance digestion.

Furthermore, it is important to have a balanced diet made up of whole grains, fresh vegetables and fruit, nuts, and healthy fats. One should also avoid processed foods, alcohol, and caffeine as they can be damaging to one's health. Additionally, 8 - 10 glasses of water throughout the day are necessary for overall health and hydration.

Finally, Ayurveda warns against eating too late in the evening, as this can interfere with the natural cleansing process of the body, depriving it of its detoxification ability. It also recommends avoiding skipping meals as this can lead to indigestion and fatigue.

In summary, foods and eating restrictions and schedules are important aspects of Ayurvedic philosophy. Eating the right foods and avoiding the wrong ones according to one's constitution will promote balance within the body and keep it functioning at its best. Eating at important times of the day and staying away from late-night eating will also promote better health. Eating the right foods in the right amount, and following an appropriate eating pattern, may help to improve and maintain health and wellbeing.

CHAPTER TWENTY-FOUR

HOME KITHCEN AND AYURVED

Spices and herbs have been an integral part of every cuisine for centuries. All over the world, different cultures have relied on these precious elements, as an important addition for both flavor and medicinal purposes. The use of spices and herbs and their health benefits has been a topic of great interest for centuries and is still a prominent topic of discussions in modern-day kitchens.

Home kitchen spices and ayurvedic food are two forms of cuisine that many individuals turn to for their properties of numerous benefits. Home kitchen spices add flavor and aroma to food, while ayurvedic food makes it easier to absorb the herbs and spices. Both forms bring multiple advantages to the table that are beneficial to overall health.

Home kitchen spices are used in almost all traditional cuisines and contain a wide variety of flavors, depending on the variety of herbs and spices that they contain. These herbs and spices differ from place-to-place and are often selected based on regional availability and taste. Common spices used in home kitchens are cumin, coriander, ginger, black pepper, cinnamon, garlic, and turmeric. Each of these brings a myriad of benefits to the table, as they not only enhance taste and aroma, but can also help with digestion, boost immunity and provide numerous other health benefits.

On the other hand, ayurveda is an ancient system of medicine from India, formulated from a combination of herbs, spices, and other ingredients. Ayurvedic food is made from highly nutritious ingredients that help balance the body's chakras, ensuring that the body functions at its optimal level. In comparison to home kitchen spices, ayurvedic food is more medicinal-oriented and can be used to cure certain ailments and promote overall health. Common ingredients used in traditional Ayurvedic dishes include shatavari, ashwagandha, Amalaki, aniseed, cardamom, and brahmi.

Although home kitchen spices bring a wonderful flavor and aroma to the table and are very beneficial in their own right; ayurvedic food makes it possible to go one step further. From aiding with digestion to improving immunity and combating inflammation, Ayurvedic food can bring a lot of value to the table, if correctly implemented in recipes.

In conclusion, spices and herbs are a vital part of any traditional cuisine and offer many health benefits. Home kitchen spices add flavor to everyday dishes, while ayurvedic food goes the extra mile, providing the body with much-needed nutrition. Both forms of cuisine have extensive advantages and should be used responsibly to ensure optimal health.

CHAPTER TWENTY-FIVE

COMMENTARIES ON AYURVEDA BY SCHOLARS AROUND THE WORLD

The ancient practice of Ayurveda stands at the heart of Indian culture, having been an essential part of understanding and health since the Vedic era. Ayurveda represents a holistic approach to health, believing in the importance of physical, mental, and spiritual balance for overall wellbeing. It is comprised of ancient texts, packed full of knowledge and commentaries from famous scholars around the world. These commentaries, ranging from simple feedback to considered research and analysis, provide valuable insight into the importance of Ayurveda and provide tangible evidence of its success in improving people's lives.

One of the most prominent scholars who have commented on Ayurveda is Pankaj Oundal, an internationally acclaimed teacher and Ayurvedic doctor. Oundal has written extensively on the importance of Ayurveda, noting its far-reaching potentials to improve physical and mental health. A key example of his writings is his commentary on the process of Ayurvedic consultations. Here, Oundal highlights the importance of a thorough holistic check-up to explore the reaction of the body to external impacts, as well as its responses to the patient's own lifestyle, diet, and mental states. In his work, Oundal also emphasises the role of the patient in the process, stressing that the management of health must involve self-awareness and self-education.

David Frawley is another renowned scholar who has devoted his time and energy to researching Ayurveda. Like Oundal, Frawley speaks to the importance of harmony within the body and of understanding Ayurveda in its broadest terms. Frawley has lent his expertise to the aid of international institutions such as the World Health Organisation in exploring the potential of Ayurveda for treating various aliments. He has also emphasised the importance of the holistic nature of Ayurveda, stressing that treatments must take into account the underlying reasons for disease, as well as the symptoms.

The importance of Ayurveda has been explored by numerous scholars around the world in both traditional and modern contexts. Vasant Lad, one such scholar, is a world-renowned teacher of Ayurvedic principles and has authored numerous books on the subject. In his writings, Lad speaks to the importance of evidence-based treatments and therapies, thus offering traditional Ayurvedic knowledge a modern footing. He is also a staunch advocate for integrative medicine, believing that modern medicine and traditional Ayurvedic practices can work together for a comprehensive approach to health.

The wealth of commentaries from world-renowned scholars on Ayurveda speaks to the effectiveness of the practice and the importance of acquiring knowledge across a range of disciplines.

SUMMARY

Ayurveda is one of the oldest holistic healing systems in the world. Originating in India more than 5,000 years ago, it is based on the idea that health and well-being depend on the proper balance of the body, mind, and spirit. This balance is achieved through the use of various natural remedies such as nutrition, herbs, yoga, and meditation.

The root of Ayurveda lies in the ancient Hindu Upanishads, which teaches that the body and mind have three distinct energies or humors, known as "doshas". Each dosha is a combination of the five fundamental elements found in the environment: air, fire, earth, water, and ether. Each element has its own unique properties such as taste, smell, temperature, form, and qualities. Depending on their relative proportion, a person's doshas are categorized as vata, pitta, or kapha. Vata is made up of air and ether and controls movement; pitta is a combination of fire and water and controls digestion and metabolism; and kapha is a combination of water and earth and is responsible for lubrication and stability.

Ayurveda attempts to maintain balance between the body and its environment by focusing on the individual's lifestyle and diet. Every individual has a unique combination of the three doshas, and the emphasis is on helping the person come back into balance by focusing on the qualities that are out of balance. To do so, Ayurveda looks at a person's diet, exercise, sleep habits, and lifestyle, in order to determine the best course of action.

Ayurveda also uses herbs, nutrition, yoga and meditation as remedies. Herbs, when combined in specific proportions, can be used as both preventative and curative agents. Nutrition is also important as it helps to cleanse the digestive tract and maintain the balance of doshas. Yoga is used to improve flexibility, strength, and mental clarity, while meditation is used to help relax the mind and reduce stress.

Ayurveda is based on the idea that disease is the result of an imbalance in the body's natural systems. By following the holistic principles of Ayurveda, people can maintain balance and improve over-all wellbeing. Ayurveda recognizes that each person is unique and should follow individualized remedies and treatments. By focusing on diet, lifestyle, and natural remedies, Ayurveda strives to maintain this balance and prevent disease from developing.

Author's Other Books

30. Rigveda in a Nutshell
31. Yajurveda in a Nutshell
32. Samveda in a Nutshell
33. Atharva Veda in a Nutshell
34. !!AYUSHMAN BHAVA!! on Ayurveda
35. Srimad Bhagavad Gita and Upanishad Connection

Contact

DR. JAGADEESH PILLAI

PhD in Vedic Science

Four Times Guinness World Record Holder

Winner of Mahatma Gandhi Vishwa Shanti Puraskar and Global Peace Ambassador

9839093003

myrichindia@gmail.com

drjagadeeshpillai@facebook

drjagadeeshpillai@instagram

jagadeeshpillai@youtube

www. JAGADEESHPILLAI.com